X   Palmer, Erin, author.
292.211 Greek mythology
PAL   BER

11-2018

GREEK MYTHOLOGY

ERIN PALMER
ILLUSTRATED BY
MATT FORSYTH

Rourke
Educational Media

rourkeeducationalmedia.com

Before & After Reading Activities

Before Reading:

Building Academic Vocabulary and Background Knowledge

Before reading a book, it is important to tap into what your child or students already know about the topic. This will help them develop their vocabulary, increase their reading comprehension, and make connections across the curriculum.

1. Look at the cover of the book. What will this book be about?
2. What do you already know about the topic?
3. Let's study the Table of Contents. What will you learn about in the book's chapters?
4. What would you like to learn about this topic? Do you think you might learn about it from this book? Why or why not?
5. Use a reading journal to write about your knowledge of this topic. Record what you already know about the topic and what you hope to learn about the topic.
6. Read the book.
7. In your reading journal, record what you learned about the topic and your response to the book.
8. After reading the book complete the activities below.

Content Area Vocabulary
Read the list. What do these words mean?

council
hearth
inspiration
offspring
pastoral
prophecy
revenge
spectacular
trident
woo

After Reading:

Comprehension and Extension Activity

After reading the book, work on the following questions with your child or students in order to check their level of reading comprehension and content mastery.

1. Name the nine muses of Greek mythology. What subject does each muse inspire? (Summarize)
2. Why did Cronus swallow his kids? (Infer)
3. Who was the god of the sea? (Asking Questions)
4. If you could be anyone from Greek mythology, who would you choose and why? (Text to Self Connection)
5. What is an example of how Greek mythology impacts modern day culture? (Asking Questions)

Extension Activity

After reading the book, choose a Greek god or goddess to learn more about. Find a story about your chosen god or goddess. Then draw your own version of the god or goddess based on the story.

Table of Contents

Chaos and Creation	4
The 12 Olympians of Mount Olympus	10
The Crazy Love Life of Zeus	16
Muses and Muscles	20
Immortal Mythology	26
Glossary	30
Index	31
Show What You Know	31
Websites to Visit	31
About the Author	32

Chaos and Creation

Passion, pain, and parties are just some parts of Greek mythology. In ancient Greece, people worshiped gods and goddesses and told epic stories of their adventures. But how did it all begin?

Ancient Greeks believed in the beginning there was nothing. They called this time of nothingness "Chaos." Then one day, it all changed.

Symbol representing Greek concept of Chaos.

Different versions of the story exist, but they often begin with Gaia, goddess of Earth, and Uranus, god of the sky. Legend says they appeared in the light one day and that was the beginning of creation.

GREAT TO CREATE
Creation myths are the stories of how life began. Almost every culture has one!

Gaia and Uranus had six sets of twins called the Titans. They also had three Cyclopes—giants with one eye in the middle of their forehead—and three other giants, each with one hundred arms and fifty heads.

Uranus wasn't fond of his **offspring**, so he tried to return them to Gaia's body, which caused her great pain. As an act of **revenge**, Gaia teamed up with Cronus, one of the Titans, to defeat Uranus.

Once Cronus was leader, he married his sister Rhea and had six children. A **prophecy** stated one of his children would overthrow him.

Because of this prophecy, every time Rhea had one of his children, Cronus would swallow the child. After this happened five times, Rhea had enough. When she gave birth to her sixth child, Zeus, she tricked her husband. Rhea wrapped a rock in a blanket. When Cronus asked for the new child, he swallowed the rock instead. Rhea sent Zeus to safety on the island of Crete.

SORRY, DAD!
Zeus later returned to defeat his father, just like the prophecy said. That's how he became the leader of the gods.

The 12 Olympians of Mount Olympus

Zeus became leader of the Olympians, a **council** of gods and goddesses who worked together to make important decisions. There were 12 Olympians, but there is disagreement about the identity of the twelfth Olympian.

WHERE MYTH AND REALITY COLLIDE

The Olympians would meet on Mount Olympus, a real place in Greece. Ancient Greek people believed their gods lived on the mountain.

These gods and goddesses made up the Olympians:

Zeus, king of the Greek gods and goddesses. He had some **spectacular** powers, including the ability to shapeshift. This means he could look like anyone or anything. Zeus was also a fierce warrior with the ability to throw lightning bolts.

Hera, queen of the Greek gods and goddesses and wife of Zeus. Hera was jealous of the other loves of Zeus. Hera and Zeus had two children together, Ares and Hephaestus.

Ares, god of war. Though he was handsome and powerful, Ares could be cruel and violent.

Poseidon, god of the sea. Poseidon and Zeus were brothers, but Poseidon never wanted to be king of the gods. Poseidon had a powerful **trident** for a weapon.

Demeter, goddess of the harvest and fertility. Zeus was Demeter's brother and he gave her the important job of keeping the crops alive so the people of Greece wouldn't starve.

Artemis, goddess of the hunt and the moon. She was the twin sister of Apollo.

Apollo, god of music. He was the son of Zeus and the goddess Leto. He also had a twin sister, Artemis. Apollo had many jobs, including making the sun come up each day.

Athena, goddess of wisdom. Her father was Zeus and her mother was his first wife, Metis.

Aphrodite, goddess of love and beauty. Some stories say she was a daughter of Zeus, others say she just appeared one day on a wave in the sea. She married Hephaestus.

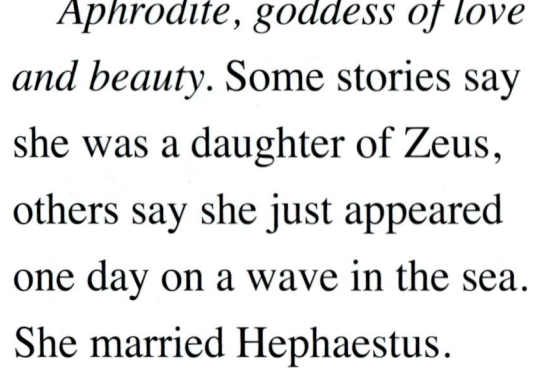

Hermes, messenger of the gods. He was the youngest son of Zeus and was a trickster.

Hestia, goddess of **hearth** *and home.* Though she was one of the original Olympians, she got sick of the fighting and gave her spot to Dionysus, the god of the vine.

Hephaestus, god of fire and forge. Some stories said he was the twelfth Olympian. Others believe it was Hades.

Hades, god of the underworld. He was the brother of Zeus and some stories claim him as the twelfth Olympian.

ORIGIN OF THE OLYMPICS

The Olympic games were inspired by the Olympians! The first Olympic games took place in ancient Greece to honor the gods.

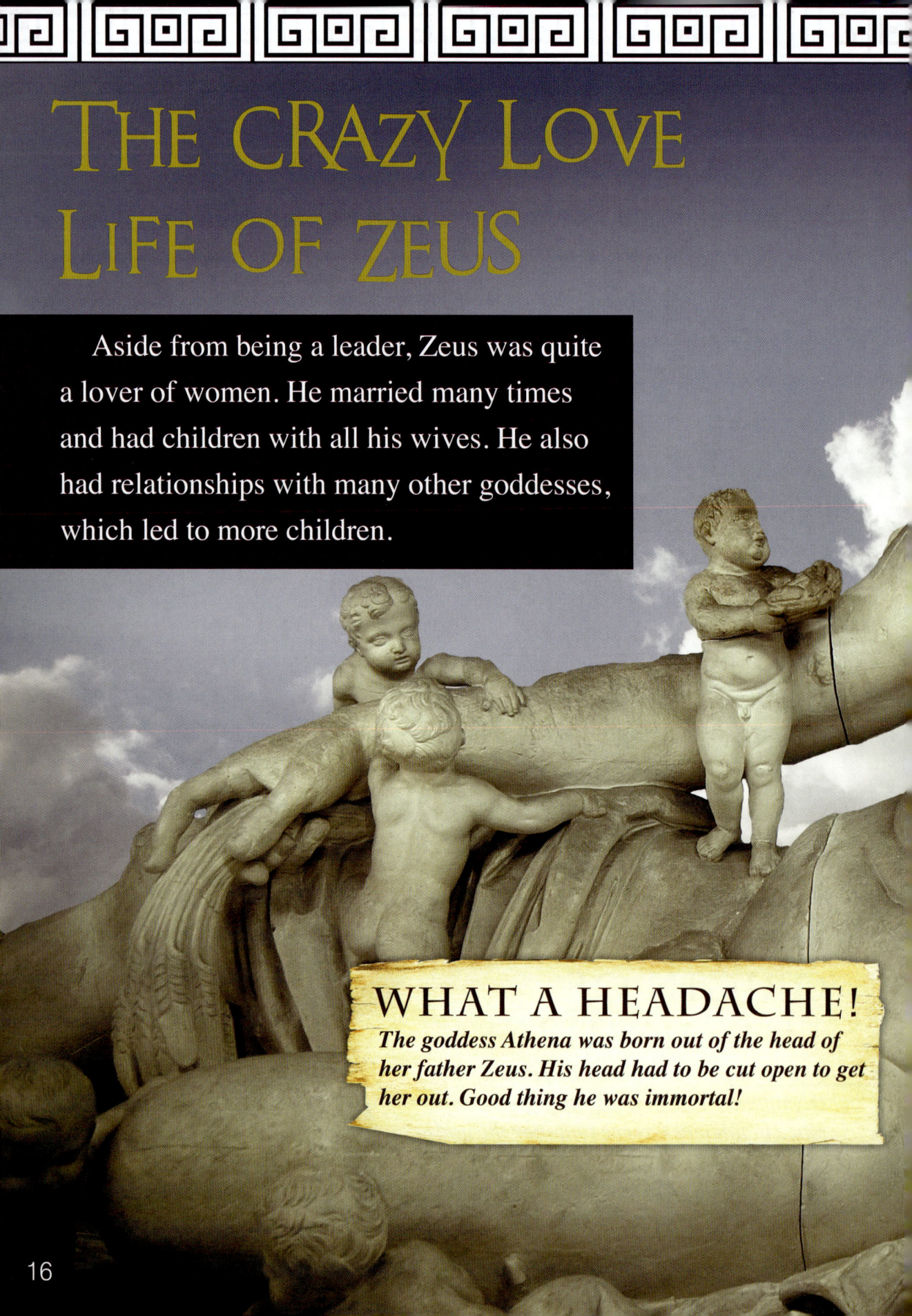

The Crazy Love Life of Zeus

Aside from being a leader, Zeus was quite a lover of women. He married many times and had children with all his wives. He also had relationships with many other goddesses, which led to more children.

WHAT A HEADACHE!
The goddess Athena was born out of the head of her father Zeus. His head had to be cut open to get her out. Good thing he was immortal!

Zeus also fell in love with many mortal women, leading to even more children. Since mortals couldn't look at gods in their true form without dying, Zeus used some interesting ways to **woo** these human women.

When Zeus fell for Leda, the human queen of Sparta, he came to her in the form of a swan. She even laid eggs when she gave birth to his children!

SEW THIS IS LOVE

Dionysus was the only god with a mortal mom. She fell in love with Zeus, saw his real form and died. Zeus saved unborn Dionysus by sewing him to his thigh.

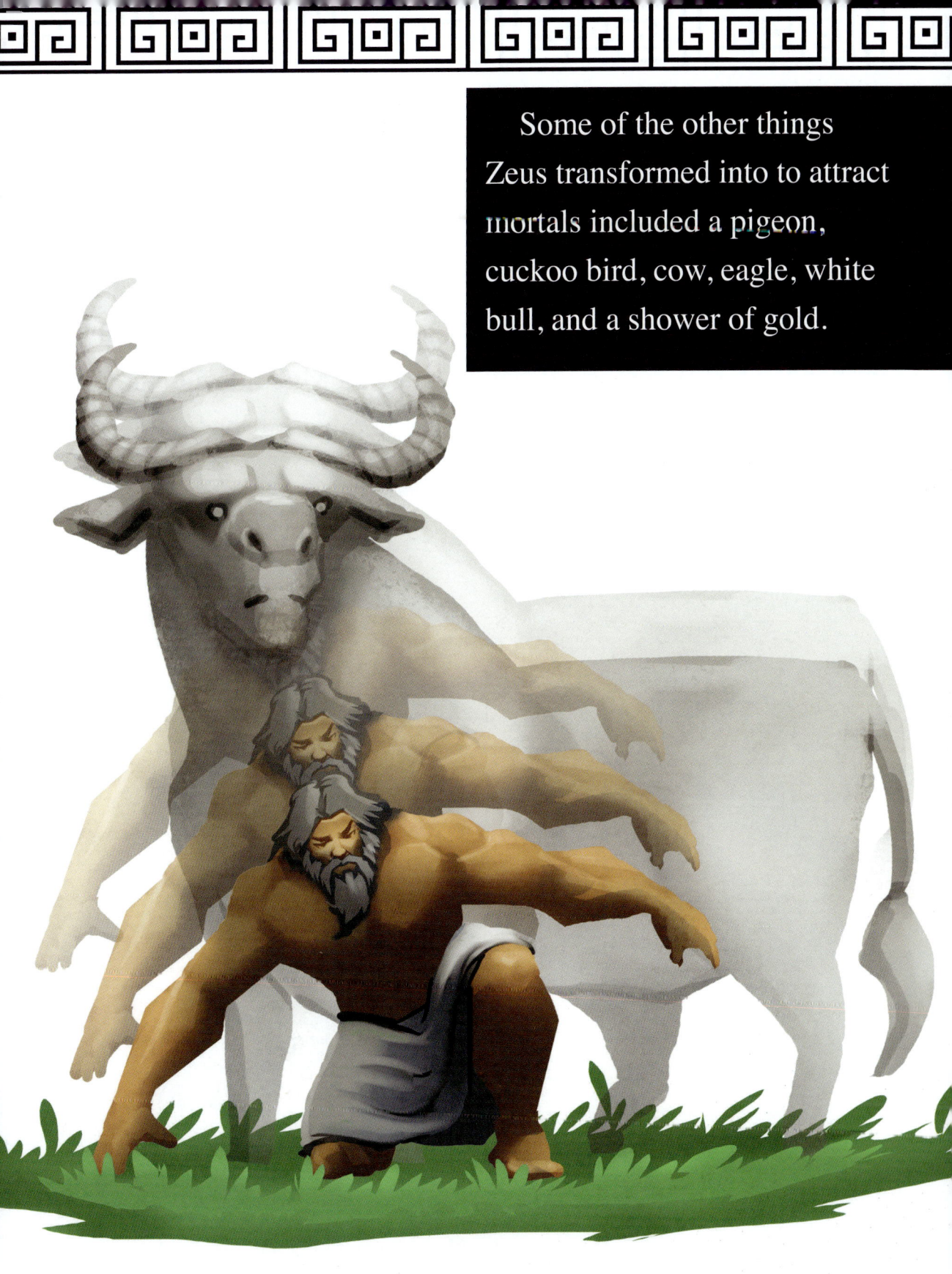

Some of the other things Zeus transformed into to attract mortals included a pigeon, cuckoo bird, cow, eagle, white bull, and a shower of gold.

MUSES AND MUSCLES

Zeus had many famous children, including some that greatly influenced Greek history. When he married Mnemosyne, the goddess of memory, she gave birth to the nine muses: goddesses of art and science.

The muses were sources of **inspiration** for human artists, musicians, poets and more. Each muse inspired a different subject:

- **Calliope** – epic poetry
- **Clio** – history
- **Euterpe** – lyric poetry
- **Thalia** – comedy and **pastoral** poetry
- **Melpomene** – tragedy
- **Terpsichore** – dance
- **Erat**o – love poetry
- **Polyhymnia** – sacred poetry
- **Urania** – astronomy

One of Zeus's most famous children was Hercules. Though he was half god and half mortal, Hercules was very strong, even as a baby.

When Hera, queen of the gods, became jealous of Hercules and sent large snakes to kill him, baby Hercules crushed the snakes and saved his own life.

Slaying the venomous Hydra was the second Labor of Hercules.

Hercules later found out he was half god and went on an epic adventure to earn the right to live on Mount Olympus with the gods.

His quest became a Greek legend that has been told for generations.

NOT EASY BEING GREEK
His journey was called the 12 Labors of Hercules. The gods gave him 12 impossible tasks to conquer, including slaying the multi-headed Hydra!

Immortal Mythology

Greek mythology went on to inspire Roman mythology, famous poems, and ancient works of literature. Some of William Shakespeare's plays and constellation names in astrology are also inspired by Greek mythology.

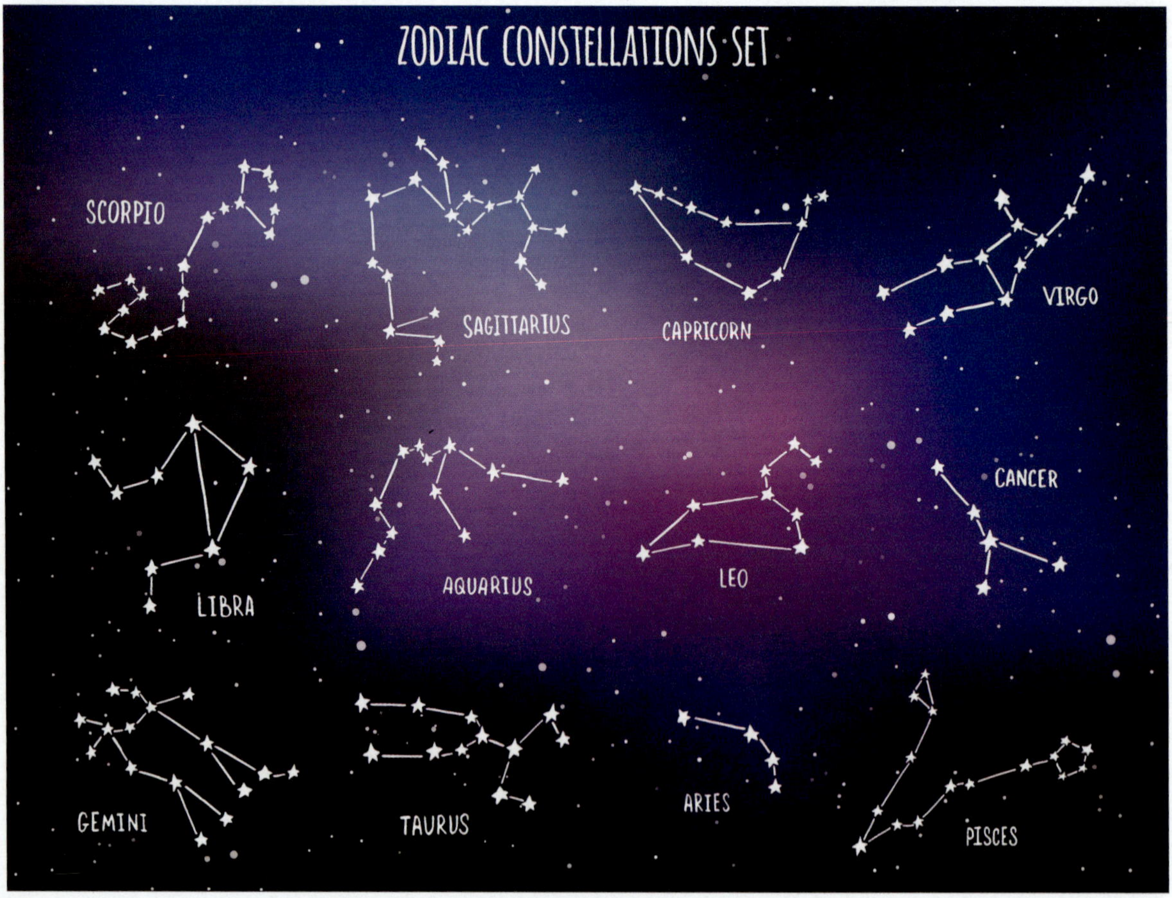

ZODIAC CONSTELLATIONS SET

Even in modern culture, there are many things inspired by Greek mythology, from movies and graphic novels to books and video games. Some brands use elements from Greek mythology in their names. Nike Inc., for example, is named after the Greek goddess of victory.

MYTH TO MOVIE
Disney made the story of Hercules into a movie. You can even see the Hercules character at Disney parks!

Greek mythology is a great example of the power of stories. One of the things that made the Greek gods and goddesses so fascinating was that they were immortal, which meant they could live forever.

Even though the gods weren't real, their tales have lasted thousands of years. So, in a way, the stories have become immortal!

GLOSSARY

council (KOUN-suhl): a group of people chosen to run a town, a county or an organization

hearth (hahrth): the floor in front of or inside a fireplace

inspiration (in-spuh-RAY-shun): the act of inspiring someone, or feeling inspired

offspring (AWF-spring): the young of an animal or human being

pastoral (PAS-tur-uhl): of or having to do with rural areas

prophecy (PRAH-fuh-see): a prediction

revenge (ri-VENJ): something you do to get back at someone for the injury or harm that the person has done to you or someone you care about

spectacular (speck-TAK-yuh-lur): remarkable or very impressive

trident (TRYE-dent): a three-pronged spear, especially as an attribute of Poseidon

woo (woo): try to gain the love of someone

Index

adventure(s) 4, 25
children 8, 9, 11, 16, 17, 18, 20, 22
giants 7
immortal 16, 28, 29
leader 8, 9, 10, 16
love(s) 11, 14, 17, 18, 21
messenger 14
mortal(s) 17, 18, 19, 22
muse(s) 20, 21
mythology 4, 26, 27, 28
shapeshift 11
stories 4, 6, 14, 15, 28, 29
twin(s) 7, 13
warrior 11

Show What You Know

1. Why was the prophecy that Cronus heard important?
2. What were some of Zeus's powers?
3. What happened to Hestia's spot as one of the 12 Olympians?
4. What were some of the ways Zeus appeared to human women?
5. How has Greek mythology affected modern culture?

Websites to Visit

www.greece.mrdonn.org
www.greekmyths4kids.com
www.historylink101.com/2/greece2

ABOUT THE AUTHOR

Erin Palmer is a writer in Tampa, Florida. She loves to read, travel and go to the beach. Erin has loved Greek mythology since she was a young girl.

Meet The Author!
www.meetREMauthors.com

© 2018 Rourke Educational Media

All rights reserved. No part of this book may be reproduced or utilized in any form or by any means, electronic or mechanical including photocopying, recording, or by any information storage and retrieval system without permission in writing from the publisher.

www.rourkeeducationalmedia.com

PHOTO CREDITS: page 3: ©Savushkin; page 4-5: ©cliffwaas; page 5, 23, 26: ©wiki; page 9: ©Zu_09; page 9(b), 15, 24-25: ©Vuk Kostic; page 10: ©Gfed; page 11: ©Sivarock; page 12: ©ieronim777; page 13: ©duncan1890; page 13(b): ©dimitrios; page 14: ©Linda Bucklin; page 15: ©Panda Vector; page 16-17: ©Fernando Cortes; page 18: ©EJDAAY; page 18(b): ©alessandro0770; page 20: ©Heritage Image Partnership Ltd; page 26: ©MsMoloko; page 27: ©DayOwl; page 27(b): ©Babi; page 28-29: ©anyaberkut

Edited by: Keli Sipperley
Illustrations by: Matt Forsyth
Cover and Interior Layout by: Rhea Magaro-Wallace

Library of Congress PCN Data

Greek Mythology / Erin Palmer
(Mythology Marvels)
ISBN 978-1-68342-357-7 (hard cover)
ISBN 978-1-68342-892-3 (soft cover)
ISBN 978-1-68342-523-6 (e-Book)
Library of Congress Control Number: 2017931268

Rourke Educational Media
Printed in the United States of America,
North Mankato, Minnesota